COUNTRY EXPLORERS

COLOMBIA

Cheryl Blackford

Lerner Publications Company • Minneapolis

Lerner Publications Company
A division of Lerner Publishing Group, Inc.
241 First Avenue North
Minneapolis, MN 55401 U.S.A.

Website address: www.lernerbooks.com

Library of Congress Cataloging-in-Publication Data

Blackford, Cheryl.
    Colombia / by Cheryl Blackford.
        p.   cm. — (Country explorers)
    Includes index.
    ISBN 978-0-7613-6417-7 (lib. bdg. : alk. paper)
    1. Colombia—Juvenile literature. I. Title.
    F2258.5.B53 2012
    986.1—dc22   2010052546

Manufactured in the United States of America
1 – MG – 7/15/11

Table of Contents

Welcome!

Colombia is one of the biggest countries on the continent of South America. Colombia has five neighbors. Panama is to the northwest. Venezuela sits to the northeast. Brazil lies to the southeast. Peru is south of Colombia. And Ecuador lies to the southwest.

The Pacific Ocean laps against Colombia's western shore. The Caribbean Sea splashes Colombia's northern beaches.

This Colombian beach faces the Caribbean Sea.

Wet or Dry?

Snowy mountains and green valleys reach from the northern to the southern borders of Colombia. In the east are flat, grassy plains, called llanos, and desert. Swamps and forests make up the Chocó. It lies near the Pacific Ocean.

The low-lying Chocó runs along the Pacific coast.

The Guajira Peninsula is a hot desert. Not many plants grow there. But the Chocó rain forest is full of plants. More than 400 inches (1,000 centimeters) of rain falls in the Chocó every year. It is one of the wettest places in the world!

Map Whiz Quiz

Look at the map on pages 4 and 5. A map is a drawing or chart of a place. Trace the outline of Colombia onto a thin sheet of paper. Can you find the Pacific Ocean? Mark it with a *W* for west. How about the Caribbean Sea? Mark it with an *N* for north. Put an *E* for east on Venezuela. Then mark Peru with an *S* for south. Color the Andes Mountains brown. Use a blue crayon to draw the rivers between the mountains.

The Guajira Peninsula is the northernmost part of South America.

7

In the Rain Forest

Rain forests are steamy hot. They flood in the rainy season. Birds and insects live in the treetops. Spider monkeys live there too.

This kind of black spider monkey is only found in Colombia and Panama.

The forest floor is dark. Tall trees block the light. You might see a jaguar. But watch out for anacondas. These giant water snakes are as long as a school bus.

Jaguars hide in the forest.

In the Mountains

Three mountain ranges form the Andes Mountains in Colombia. The ranges are the Occidental (West), the Central, and the Oriental (East). Between the ranges are long valleys with rich farmland. The Cauca and Magdalena rivers flow through these valleys.

This Andean valley has rich farmland.

Cristóbal Colón is the highest mountain in Colombia. The mountain is named after the explorer Christopher Columbus.

The Moving Earth

The Andes Mountains are a huge wrinkle on Earth's crust. The crust is Earth's outside layer. The crust is divided into pieces called plates. The plates fit together like giant puzzle pieces. They move and push against one another. The mountains formed when plates pushed together.

This view from Cristóbal Colón shows the tall mountains in the northern part of Colombia.

Deadly Volcanoes

Some of Colombia's mountains are volcanoes. And some of those volcanoes still erupt, or blow up. When the Ruiz volcano erupted in 1985, the snow and ice on top of it melted. The water mixed with ash from the volcano. It made a huge river of mud that buried the town of Armero.

This picture from 1985 shows the damage from the Ruiz volcano eruption.

Galeras is Colombia's most active volcano. In 1993, an eruption killed nine people. Galeras erupted twice in 2010. But no one was hurt.

Record Holder

Colombia has the tallest palm trees in the world. You'll also find more kinds of orchid plants than anywhere else.

Colombia has more kinds of lizards, toads, and frogs than any other country. And it has more kinds of birds than anywhere else in the world. Colombia is a record breaker in many ways!

Don't Eat Me!

If you see a tiny, golden frog in the rain forest, don't touch it! It might be a poison dart frog. The bright color is a warning. Hunters use the poison from its skin on their blowgun darts. When the dart pokes an animal, the animal dies.

Chemicals on the skin of poison dart frogs are dangerous to animals.

First Peoples

Native people have lived in Colombia for thousands of years. The Muisca people were farmers in the Andes Mountains. They lived in round homes made of sticks and clay. Not many Muisca people are left in modern-day Colombia.

El Dorado

Each new leader of the Muisca people covered himself in gold dust. Then he dove from a raft in Lake Guatavita in central Colombia to wash off the gold. His people threw gold and emeralds into the water. The Spanish name for the golden man was *El Dorado*. No one has ever found the gold and jewels in the lake. But more than five hundred years ago, Muisca people made this copy of the raft in gold.

The Wayuu people still live in the Guajira desert. They keep cattle and goats. They move around to find food and water. Some of them work in the salt mines to earn money. Small groups of native people live in the rain forest. They hunt, fish, and travel in canoes.

These women are working in the salt mines on the Guajira Peninsula.

Strangers in the Land

In the 1500s, explorers sailed from Spain to Colombia. They fought the native people and won. The Spanish then ruled Colombia for three hundred years.

Gonzalo Jiménez de Quesada was a Spanish explorer of Colombia. He founded Bogotá in 1538.

The Spanish explorers sent Colombian gold to Spain. Their ships sailed from the city of Cartagena. The Spanish built forts and strong walls around Cartagena.

Hi Pops,

I'm having fun in Cartagena. Today we went to Fort San Felipe. That's a big fort outside the old city walls. The walls are as tall as a building with three floors. I pretended I was a Spanish soldier marching on the walls. Tomorrow we're going to the beach. I'm going to swim in the Caribbean Sea. Mom says I can look for sea turtles.

Love,
Sam

Fort San Felipe

Free People

Colombians began to fight for their freedom in the late 1700s. They fought against Spanish rule. They finally won independence in 1819.

This engraving from the 1800s shows the Battle of Boyaca. This battle led to Colombian independence in 1819.

Some Spanish settlers married native people. Their children were called mestizos. More than half of modern-day Colombians are mestizos. The Spanish brought African slaves to Colombia. Other settlers came from countries such as Germany and France. Many Colombians are a mix of these people.

What's Your Name?

People in Colombia often have two last names. Their first last name is the same as their father's. And their second last name is the same as their mother's. Pretend your name is Juan Pablo García Rodríguez. Then your dad's last name is García, and your mom's is Rodríguez.

This woman and her daughter are mestizos.

City Life

Most people in Colombia live in crowded cities like Bogotá and Medellín. Bogotá has about five million people.

22

Bogotá is in central Colombia.

In Bogotá, wealthy and middle-class people have comfortable houses or apartments. Poor people live in run-down buildings or in shacks made of cardboard or tin. The shacks often don't have electricity. Many of the poor people come from the country to find work in the city.

This area of Bogotá is crowded with shacks.

Country Life

People who live in the country are called campesinos.
Campesinos might work all day on farms or in mines.
At home, they grow food and make clothes for their families.

These men work on a
banana plantation, or farm,
in northern Colombia.

24

Campesino children gather wood for fires to cook meals.
If their home doesn't have water, they fetch it from a well.
Sometimes they are too busy helping out to go to school.

Children who live in the country usually help with the family's farmwork.

Getting Around

Colombia's mountains, swamps, and forests once made it hard to get around. But modern-day Colombians can travel on roads or in planes. In Colombia's big cities, people can ride buses, trains, or taxis. In Medellín, cable cars take people around.

A cable car gives people a way to ride up the mountain in Medellín.

26

Chivas are common in the countryside. These are buses with wooden benches and open sides. They are painted in bright colors. When the bus is full, people sit on the roof!

School

Colombian children start primary school when they are six. They learn to read and write. They study math and science too. And they learn about music, art, and religion. When they are twelve, they go to secondary school.

Most children in Colombia wear uniforms to school.

Colombian parents might pay for their children to go to a private school. Public schools are free. But sometimes public schools don't have enough books or teachers. Then some children go to school in the morning. Others go in the afternoon.

Some people in Colombia also go on to study in college.

Religion

Most Colombians are Roman Catholic. The Spanish settlers brought this religion to Colombia. Important religious days, such as Christmas and Easter, are national holidays.

These people are walking in an Easter parade in north central Colombia.

Many tourists visit Zipaquirá each year.

Holy Week is the week before Easter. During Holy Week, Colombians carry figures of holy people through the streets in parades.

Church of Salt

At Zipaquirá, a very special church lies deep underground in a salt mine. First, miners dug out the salt. Then they carved a church in the cave. If you touch the wall and lick your finger, you can taste the salt.

Let's Eat

In the mountains, what could be better than a bowl of soup? *Ajiaco de pollo* is a thick soup made with chicken, potatoes, and corn.

This family is sharing a large bowl of soup.

On a hot day near the ocean, try some *arroz con coco*. That's rice with coconut. Eat it with fish for your evening meal.

Snack Time

It's snack time. How about some crunchy fried ants? That's a treat in parts of Colombia! Empanadas are popular everywhere. Empanadas are pastries filled with meat and vegetables. Bunuelos are tasty doughnuts made from corn flour and cheese.

These bunuelos have cinnamon sticks on top. They are a great sweet treat.

Coffee

Many people around the world drink coffee. And a lot of that coffee comes from Colombia.

This man is picking ripe coffee beans from a coffee plant.

Coffee farmers do all their work by hand. They can't use machines on the hills where the coffee trees grow. Even the coffee beans must be picked by hand. One coffee tree grows enough coffee beans each year to make about forty cups of coffee.

Flowers

Colombia is number two in the world for selling fresh flowers. Only the Netherlands, a country in Western Europe, sells more. Colombia's flowers are shipped throughout the world.

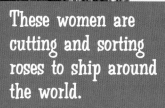

These women are cutting and sorting roses to ship around the world.

Underground Riches

Colombians have mined emeralds for hundreds of years. The miners dig tunnels and search riverbeds for these stones. When miners find emeralds, they are green lumps. But when emeralds are cut, they sparkle.

This emerald has been cut so that it shines.

Some of the world's finest emeralds come from Colombia.
Workers also mine gold, silver, copper, and salt in Colombia.

These men work in an emerald mine in north central Colombia.

Beautiful Things

Long ago, the native people of Colombia made beautiful things from gold. They crafted fine stone figures and pots. Modern-day Colombians make leather goods and colorful cloth. They create baskets too.

Many people sell the goods they make at small shops in city markets.

Gabriel García Márquez is a famous Colombian writer. He is one of the best-known writers in the world.

Fernando Botero is an artist from Colombia. He paints pictures and creates sculptures of chubby people.

Gabriel García Márquez won the Nobel Prize for Literature in 1982.

Music and Dance

Most Colombians love music, singing, and dancing. *Cumbia* music is lively. It copies the beat of the music brought by African slaves. The musicians play drums and pipes. They might also play a rattle called a maraca.

Cumbia dancing is lively too. If you want to learn cumbia, find a partner. Then get ready for some fancy footwork!

Shakira performs all over the world.

Shakira

Shakira is a famous Colombian singer and dancer. Shakira wrote the official song for the 2010 World Cup soccer tournament. The song is called "Waka, Waka (This Time for Africa)." Millions of people around the world watched her sing it.

Sports

Colombians are wild about soccer. They call it *fútbol*. They watch soccer games on television. They dance and cheer when their team wins. Carlos Valderrama is a famous Colombian soccer player. His nickname is El Pibe (the kid). He played for teams in Colombia, France, and the United States.

Carlos Valderrama played professional soccer in the United States from 1996 to 2004.

Colombian soccer players celebrate a goal against Paraguay during a match in 2011.

Bullfighting is popular in parts of Colombia. Cities like Bogotá
and Medellín have big bullrings. Matadors fight bulls in them.

THE FLAG OF COLOMBIA

Colombia's flag has yellow, blue, and red stripes across it. The yellow stripe is as big as the blue and red stripes together. People have different ideas about what the colors mean. Many people think the yellow stripe stands for the gold found in Colombia. The blue stripe makes people think of Colombia's rivers and seas. The red stripe represents the blood of the people who died for Colombia's independence.

FAST FACTS

FULL COUNTRY NAME: Republic of Colombia

AREA: about 440,000 square miles (1,139,000 square kilometers), or about twice the size of the state of Texas

MAIN LANDFORMS: the mountain ranges Andes, Occidental, Central, Oriental and the Sierra Nevada de Santa Marta; the Guajira Peninsula; the valleys Cauca and Magdalena; the Pacific lowlands; the Llanos grasslands and forested plains

MAJOR RIVERS: Amazon, Arauca, Caquetá, Cauca, Magdalena, Meta, Putumayo, and San Juan

ANIMALS AND THEIR HABITATS: anteaters, eagles, condors, hummingbirds, spectacled bears, tapirs (mountains), bats, butterflies, capybaras, frogs, insects, jaguars, macaws, mice, parrots, snakes, spider monkeys, tamarin monkeys, toucans (rain forest), turtles (ocean), armadillos, iguanas, snakes, tortoises (desert), herons, storks (lakes), capybaras (grasslands), caimans, catfish, crocodiles, pink dolphins, piranhas (rivers)

CAPITAL CITY: Bogotá

OFFICIAL LANGUAGE: Spanish

POPULATION: about 43,000,000

GLOSSARY

campesino: a person who lives in the country

desert: a place that gets hardly any rain

emerald: a sparkly, green stone used to decorate things like rings and necklaces

erupt: to blow up, or pour out of the ground

fort: a place protected by strong walls and ditches. Forts might have soldiers living in them.

map: a drawing or chart of all or part of Earth or the sky

matador: a bullfighter who kills bulls in a bullring

mestizo: the Spanish word for mixed; a person who has a mixed Spanish and native background

peninsula: a piece of land with water almost all the way around it

TO LEARN MORE

BOOKS

Donaldson, Madeline. *South America.* Minneapolis: Lerner Publications Company, 2005. Explore other places on the continent of South America.

Walker, Sally. *Volcanoes.* Minneapolis: Lerner Publications Company, 2008. This book has great photos and lots of fun, interesting facts about volcanoes.

Watson, Galadriel. *Natural Wonders: The Amazon Rain Forest.* New York: Weigl Publishers, 2005. Find out more about the Amazon rain forest.

WEBSITES

Kids Monga Bay
http://kids.mongabay.com/
See lots of colorful photos of rain forest animals and plants.

National Geographic: Colombia
http://travel.nationalgeographic.com/travel/countries/colombia-guide/
Read facts about Colombia. Watch a video of the salt cathedral at Zipaquirá.

Rain Forest Alliance
http://www.rainforest-alliance.org/education.cfm?id=kidsmain
This website has fun activities to help you learn about the rain forest.

INDEX